WESLEY PAUL, MARATHON RUNNER

Wesley Paul, Marathon Runner

by Julianna A. Fogel

Photographs by Mary S. Watkins

J. B. Lippincott   New York

Thanks to Carl Charleson, who got us around the
Big Apple; Tom Johnston, and his motorcycle at 6:00 A.M.;
Wilma Yeo, who encouraged us; Jerry, who
ran first; Curt, who is definitely a long-distance runner;
and the Paul family, especially our new friend Wesley.

Photograph on page 33 by William S. Lonsdale.

A portion of the proceeds from this book goes
to the Columbia, Missouri, Track Club to help
fund a running program for children.

Designed by Kohar Alexanian

First Edition

U.S. Library of Congress Cataloging in Publication Data
Fogel, Julianna A
    Wesley Paul, marathon runner.
    SUMMARY: Highlights the life of a Chinese
American runner, his record-breaking performance
in the New York City Marathon at the age of nine,
and his dream to compete in the Olympics.
    1. Paul, Wesley—Juvenile literature.
2. Runners (Sports)—United States—Biography—
Juvenile literature. 3. Marathon running—
Juvenile literature. [1. Paul, Wesley.
2. Track and field athletes. 3. Chinese
Americans—Biography] I. Watkins, Mary S.
II. Title.
GV697.W44F63   796.4'26   [B][92] 78-23649
ISBN-0-397-31845-6   ISBN-0-397-31861-8 (LB)

For Brooke, Courtney, Paul, and Tuc,
champions at giving, sharing, understanding, loving

My name is Wesley Paul. I'm nine years old. When I was three, my dad started jogging to lose weight, and he took me along. I've been running ever since.

At first, I ran just for fun. I didn't keep track of how far or how fast I could go. But then I began to enjoy doing a little better each time, and I got serious about it.

A lot of kids can run fast for short distances, but running long distances is really different from sprints across the playground. You have to train, build your endurance and strength. I run at least ten miles every day.

The kids in my class ask me to race at recess, but I try to
get out of it, because I'm kind of shy and I don't want to
make a big deal of my running. It's better if I stick to
four-square, where we can all have fun.

3

When I get home from school, I have a glass of milk and talk to my mother and my brother Darcy. Darcy is two. Sometimes he comes out and tries to run with me, but he can't keep up because he's still too little. If he was closer to my age, we could do more things together.

After my snack, I change my clothes and get ready to work out.

4

First, I warm up with twenty or
thirty different stretch exercises—
some to the side, some forward;
some standing, some sitting. There
seems to be an exercise for every
single muscle. Doing them isn't
much fun, but it's important. One
time when I didn't warm up before
running, I pulled a muscle. I
couldn't run for four days.

5

I work out every day, winter and summer. The only time I get bored is when the weather is really bad and I have to run indoors. It's easy to lose count of my distance when I'm going around and around on the same flat track.

My dad is my coach. He decides which races I should enter, and he plans all my training. He maps different routes for me and clocks my workouts with a stopwatch.

Mostly I train on a golf course, which is pretty flat. Some days Dad has me run hills. Hills can be killers for a runner, but I try to think of them as friends. They are great for building up your legs and wind. Many runners can't keep their pace going uphill, so hills can be great places to pass other runners in races.

The longest race I run is the marathon. A long time ago, in Greece, a soldier ran to Athens from another city called Marathon to bring news of his army's victory. The marathon is the same distance that soldier ran—26 miles, 385 yards. So far, I have run in seven marathons.

9

One week before I run a marathon, I run 20 miles without stopping. If I can run that far, I know I'll be able to run 26 miles, 385 yards—or even farther. I got lost once during a marathon, and when I finally found the finish line I learned I had covered 33 miles. Boy, was I mad!

Once, the summer I was eight, I had to drop out of a marathon—but that was because I was hit by a car. At the 6-mile mark, the car's outside mirror slammed into me.

I had trained for that race all summer, hoping to break the national record for eight-year-olds. I wanted to keep going, but I couldn't. The stitches I got in the back of my head didn't hurt nearly as much as the disappointment inside.

My dad knew how I felt. He said, "Wesley, if you recover in time, we'll enter the Mayor Daley Marathon in Chicago."

I wasn't so sure how I would do in Chicago. I had never run in a marathon in a big city. The race was only two weeks away, and I couldn't train for it because of the accident.

I did okay. I finished 250th out of 5,000 runners, and I won a trophy for my age division. But I didn't break the record for eight-year-olds.

After the Chicago race, I felt kind of let down. I kept thinking, "I could have broken that record, if only I hadn't been hit by that dumb car."

About two weeks later, I got an invitation to run in the New York City Marathon. I was very excited about it. Runners don't usually get special invitations to be in a race; they just sign up. I was invited because I had done well in Chicago. The New York race is really big and important. Best of all, it was another chance for me to break the national record.

14

Before the race, my dad gave me last-minute instructions. He reminded me that my time would be called out at the mile markers and told me to listen so I would know if I was keeping my pace up. Then he said, "I think you will break that record today."

And I did! I ran the marathon in 3 hours, 31 seconds. I broke the record by 15 whole minutes.

Before long, I began thinking about running a marathon even faster. During the whole next year I worked to build up my speed and strength. I ran in a lot of shorter races and trained hard.

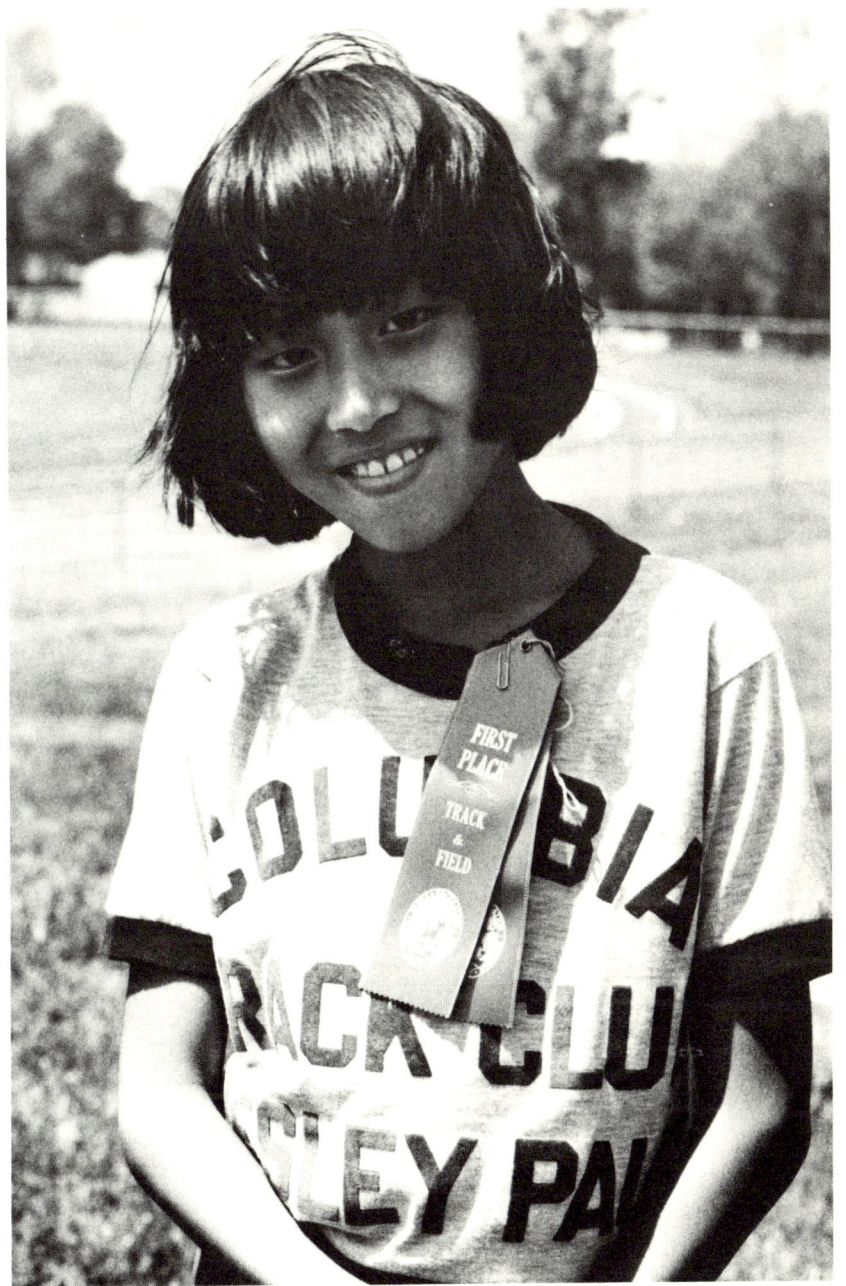

All my training was aimed at a new goal: to finish a marathon in under three hours.

I had been looking forward to the New York City Marathon for weeks. I guess that's why I was so nervous. The race wasn't supposed to begin until 10:30 in the morning, but I made sure we were there by 7:00.

I was worried about the weather. Perfect weather for running a marathon is between 40 and 50 degrees Fahrenheit, and cloudy. But the forecast was for 75 degrees and sunny. It's awful to run when it's hot, because your body loses so much liquid when you perspire.

I checked my socks and shoes very carefully. I made sure that my heels were all the way back in the shoes and that there were no wrinkles in the socks, so I wouldn't get blisters. I tied the laces in double knots. Something was doing the same to my stomach.

Then I did stretch exercises for about an hour. I kept remembering the dream I had had the night before. It was terrible. I was running in the New York City Marathon. It was boiling hot, and I quit at the 5-mile mark. My time was three hours, but I had gone only five miles. All the runners were dropping out, as if we were all under a spell....

23

I wished there was a machine with a switch I could turn to control the weather.

24

Lots of runners meditate before a race. Some people try
to make their minds go blank. But I think about the race,
every single step. I think about my pace and about how
I'm going to breathe, and I imagine how I will feel at the
5-mile mark... the 15... the 20. I run the whole race in
my mind, if I can.

An older kid came up and asked me, "What's your time going to be?"

I said, "Less than three hours."

He said, "You're kidding."

I told him I wasn't.

Then he asked me for advice, because he'd never run in a marathon before.

Big city… big race… big butterflies!
The worst part of a marathon is
standing around waiting. It seemed
like forever before the starting
cannon went off.

27

Boom! I heard something else that sounded like a huge roar, but it was just the crowd cheering.

We started up slowly. There were so many runners I could hardly move.

After about two miles, the runners finally began to spread out. I didn't feel so crowded, and running was easier.

Some runners hold back at the start of a marathon because they are afraid they'll get tired too quickly. I've never done that. I try to keep my pace steady.

In order to break three hours, I had to run each mile of the marathon in 6 minutes, 30 seconds.

The next ten miles clicked off fast. It was pretty quiet. Some of the runners were talking back and forth, but I didn't talk to anyone. I just listened to the sound of other runners breathing and shoes thumping on the pavement, and concentrated on my pace.

I had lots of time to think. I thought about music and made up tunes and hummed them. I worked math problems in my head; I took the number of miles I had run and multiplied it by six and one-half, to keep track of how much time should have passed.

By the 15-mile mark, I was hot and thirsty. My legs had begun to feel sore, as if some invisible hammer was hitting them. I thought, "I still have over eleven miles to go."

Then some boy yelled, "Hey, kid! What are you doing in this race? You'll never make it. Why don't you just quit now?"

He did me a real favor. He made me more determined than ever to break three hours.

Lots of runners talk about "hitting the wall" during a marathon. It means reaching a point where all your energy is gone and you feel as if you're trying to run through a brick wall. It usually happens sometime during the last six miles.

I hit the wall at the 22-mile mark. All of a sudden, I felt as if I couldn't take another step. That's what it must be like to be zapped by a laser gun. I felt paralyzed.

All around me, runners were dropping out, just like in my dream. I thought, "I can't move." But somehow I kept going.

At the 25-mile mark, I heard the crowd yelling. This time
it was encouragement: "C'mon! You can do it! Go!"
I told myself, "Wesley, you're almost finished. Run!"

33

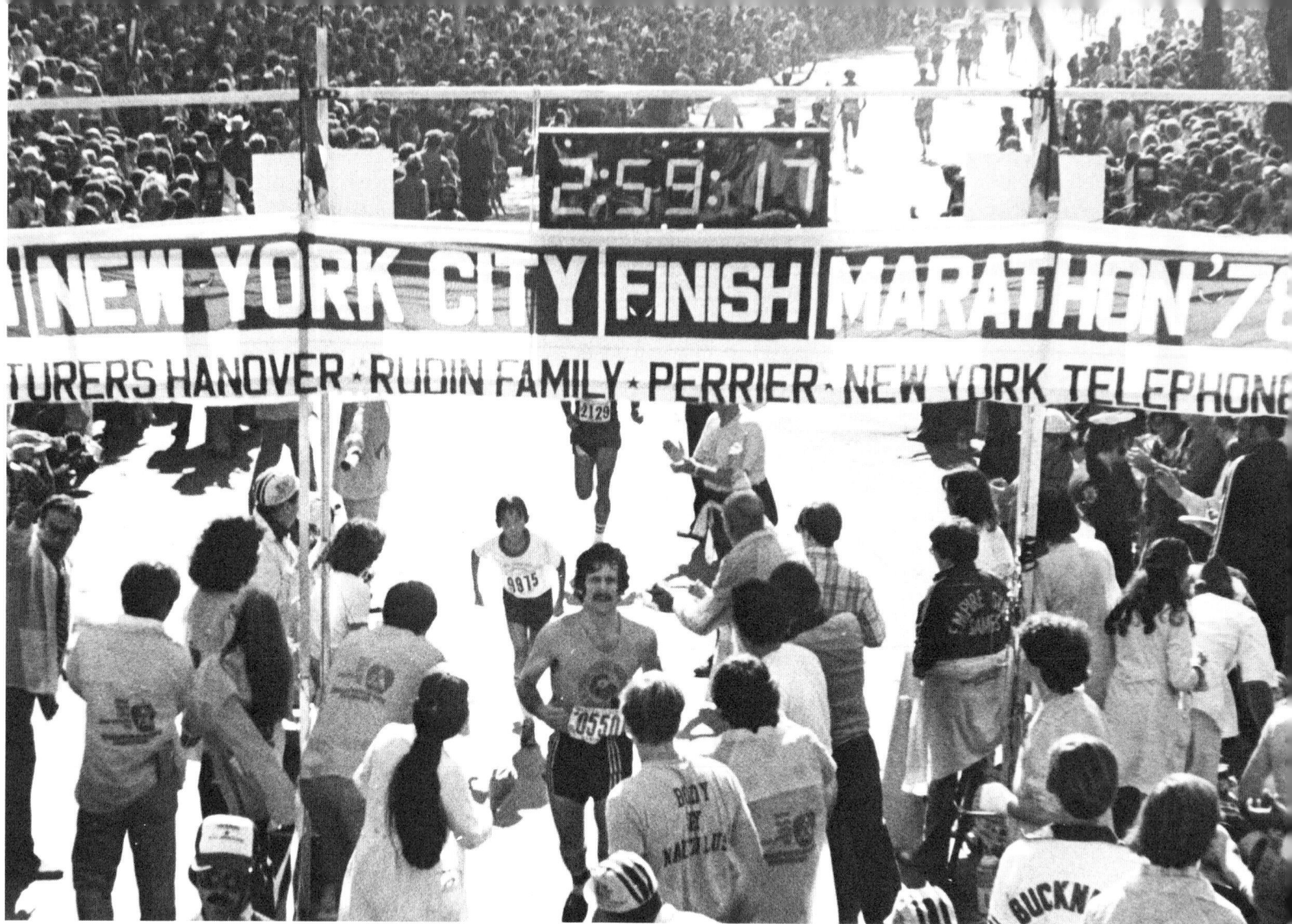

Soon I could see the big clock at the finish line. When I got close enough to read what it said, I couldn't believe it.

Two hours, 59 minutes!

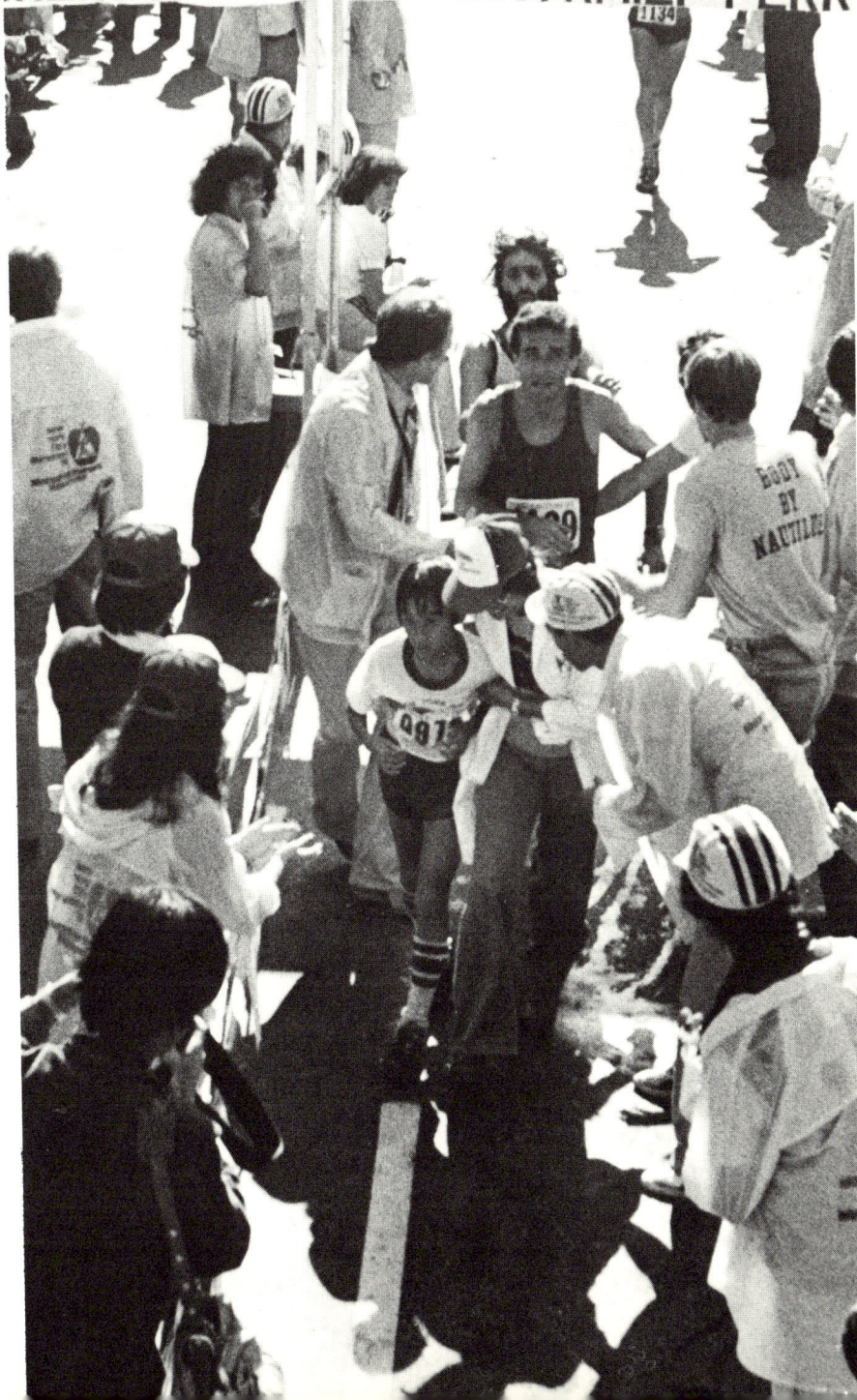

As I crossed the finish line, somebody rushed up to me, handed me a medal, and said, "Good job!"

All the months of training had paid off. In spite of the heat, I had broken three hours.

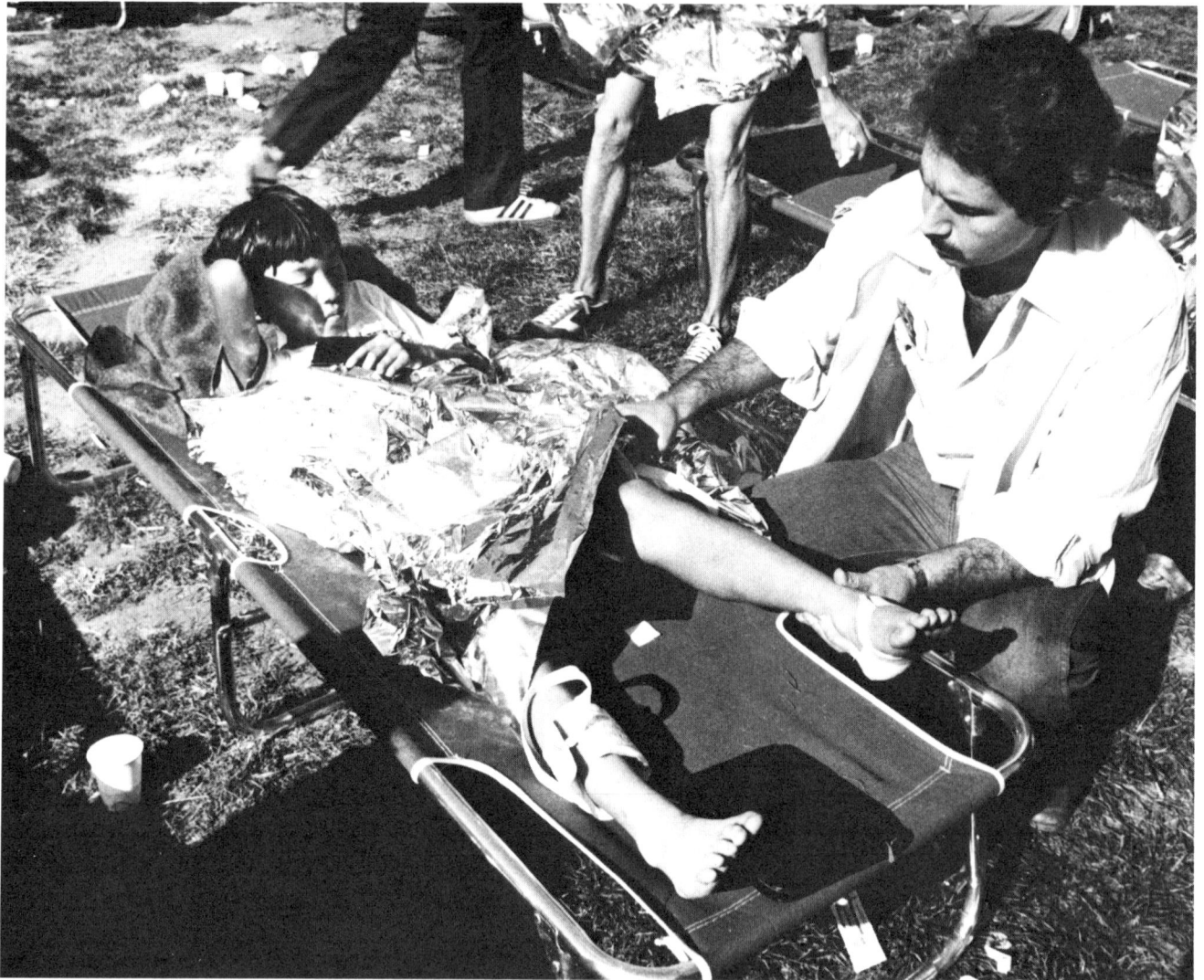

All the runners who finished were wrapped in foil so we wouldn't cool off too quickly. I was so tired it seemed unreal. And I had gotten a big blister after all.

But it felt wonderful to have reached my goal.

Of course, there's always another race to win, another record to break—even if it's your own.

What I really want to do is try out for the Olympics when I'm old enough.

But there is more to running than winning races and breaking records. Running is fun. It makes you feel good. You can run with a friend, or go alone if you feel like being by yourself. You can set your own pace. And you don't need a lot of equipment.

38

All you have to do is walk out the door and start.

39

About the Author and Photographer

Julianna A. Fogel has a bachelor's degree in journalism from the University of Missouri. She lives in Kansas City, Missouri, with her husband and two children. Besides writing, Ms. Fogel's interests include travel, skiing, and running.

Mary S. Watkins has worked in education and in public relations. She is currently a free-lance photographer and printmaker. She and her husband have two children and live in Mission, Kansas.

Ms. Fogel and Ms. Watkins have been friends since college. WESLEY PAUL, MARATHON RUNNER is their first book.